GW01099271

MOTION PHOTOS

poems by

Nina Bannett

Finishing Line Press
Georgetown, Kentucky

MOTION PHOTOS

Copyright © 2024 by Nina Bannett
ISBN 979-8-88838-570-8 First Edition
All rights reserved under International and Pan-American Copyright Conventions.
No part of this book may be reproduced in any manner whatsoever without written permission from the publisher, except in the case of brief quotations embodied in critical articles and reviews.

Publisher: Leah Huete de Maines
Editor: Christen Kincaid
Cover Art: Mary Ann Biehl
Author Photo: Brad Fox
Cover Design: Elizabeth Maines McCleavy

Order online: www.finishinglinepress.com
also available on amazon.com

Author inquiries and mail orders:
Finishing Line Press
PO Box 1626
Georgetown, Kentucky 40324
USA

Contents

Adaptation 1

Diagnosis 12

Motion Photos 13

Scorecard 14

Hymn 15

Northeast Regional 156 16

Layout 17

Recurring Dream... 18

For my father and his trains

Adaptation

HE NEVER BROKE but
always fell in multiples,
columns of numbers
through an adding machine,
greeting emergency as
only economy since so many
falls amounted to nothing.

ALL OVER THE WALLS are motion.
Trains are distractions.
Eliminate the motion.
This will help him move.

A MAN CAN get through
his doorway with his ego.
Maneuver space to fit challenges.
Widen narrow.

NO ONE WANTS IT, the bottom
of this barrel where the floor is thick
and he can make his own laws.

NOT ME. Superfluous
articles and prepositions.
Always better to supply
less required space.

HE HOLDS his ground.
Until they return
six times a day
lifting him off the floor.

HE REMEMBERS his futures.
Slips being read out loud
through his daughter's brown eyes.

HE DOES NOT want to
become a cyborg.
An iron horse is honor.
It moves him.

SCANT OPTIONS in mean country.
Swamp will swallow him
even in one bedroom.

LESS FOOD and more water is healthier. Marsh is sacred ground, a digging in when there are no days out.

TRAINS CANNOT RUN
Stuck in the marsh
of the brain. If a man is well made,
he should last a lifetime.

Diagnosis

Prepare to hold syntax.

punctuate steps, with such halt
that if it were poetic meter,
it would be   spondee,

no sense emphasis
no hope emphasis

iambic pentameter recedes
into abnormal eye movements
non-vertical and non-linear

the wheel running over his brain

why try too hard
to understand the rhythm
when it is so rare

Motion Photos

Past liberty comes in
packs of likeminded men
in search of steam engines.
Photos hurtle forward into
their railfan cameras.

The new neurologist
showcases patient footage
at his team meeting
backs up his legs again and again
as they choke through each step.

Scorecard

A clipboard won't be enough
to record his losses. No template for
watching himself going backwards,
against a merciless ball
tarred with tau proteins
too slippery to grasp.

Hymn

May he walk. Claim his cyborg.
Restore legs.

May he balance. Rise to challenge.
Restore balance.

May he swim. Clutch bottom.
Restore backstroke.

May he filter. Purify.
Restore kidneys.

May he eat devotional toast.
Restore swallow.

May he swallow.

May he shadow.

May he swan.

Northeast Regional 156

in a window seat   in an exit row
I spy a freight yard, and the only time

I've ever cried at something so boring
I broke down like   a train

silent, unmoving and so   *loved*

the ones he loved   the most
except his daughter

between an Amtrak seat   and the window

and I broke down   like a train
in one place

popular route   unpopular time,
home train   grief train

I will never   forget my father
or the April wakeup   call this morning

automated voice   telling me   *the weather for January 16*
is thirty-two degrees with a chance of light snow

typical forecast atypical time
home time   grief time   cruelest

Layout

Letters and paperwork.
Choosing sayings,
names. Carving
him into dark
marble block solid,
tears backed into a corner
where streetlights
don't plan on being lit
any time soon. All I have
to do is send one more
check but all I can do
is stick the stamp on,
finger my pen, rendering
like bone, look out
for a train ready to run
me over, push me to jump
onto the tracks as I
learn the grip of being
a daughter putting a world
on a stone set to breathe
only when visitors come.

Recurring Dream

technical and grey,
serial numbered
passenger cars,
hoppers, loads of coal
N scale but full size

freight yards with boxcars
like fields of flowers
flowing from tracks
familiar species,
phlox, forget-me-nots
spanning the yard
fanning fires
of time and love,
in Morristown
or Sault Saint Marie,
or the Sunnyside yard,

those engines of ghosts,
live steam, coal-fired,
my dream a dire hobo,
to tramp around
the muddy ground,
those trains a soft bouquet,
flowers I hand you,

tied in electrical wire,
restless, our palms
cherry blossoms,
and the ties run over
both our twenty fingers,
veins, knuckles,
ducking the current,
wondering how
trains can do all this.

Nina Bannett is the author of *These Acts of Water* (ELJ Publications 2015) and a chapbook, *Lithium Witness* (Finishing Line Press, 2011). Her poetry has been featured in numerous journals including *North American Review, Valley Voices, Bellevue Literary Review* and *WomenArts Quarterly*. She is Professor of English at New York City College of Technology, City University of New York where she teaches writing and literature courses. In addition to publishing poetry, Nina has published academic articles on American women writers including Mary Austin, Elizabeth Stoddard, Harriet Beecher Stowe, Cheryl Strayed, and Edith Wharton. She lives and writes in Brooklyn.
www.ninabannett.com

Milton Keynes UK
Ingram Content Group UK Ltd.
UKHW011120050624
443649UK00006B/419